To my young self, you are not a loser.

# Maha Badawaki

# RHYTHM RESONANCE

AUSTIN MACAULEY PUBLISHERS™

LONDON • CAMBRIDGE • NEW YORK • SHARJAH

ISBN – 9789948789284 – (Paperback)
ISBN – 9789948789291 – (E-Book)

Application Number: MC-10-01-2513746
Age Classification: E

Printer Name: iPrint Global Ltd
Printer Address: Witchford, England

First Published 2023
AUSTIN MACAULEY PUBLISHERS FZE
Sharjah Publishing City
P.O Box [519201]
Sharjah, UAE
www.austinmacauley.ae
+971 655 95 202

# Intro

*In this book, you'll believe in the reciprocity of human feelings.*

*You'll believe in the commonality of our suffering exhilaration, vulnerability, and affection regardless of our various background narratives.*

*In this book you'll believe in your strengths, you'll embrace your insecurities, and reattach to your inner soul.*

*In this book you'll resonate with me, yourself, and the others.*

*In this book, I'll be naked and exposed, yet no shame is going to be involved.*

# Dreamy

*She is the next-door girl*
*Wearing a skirt with a swirl*
*So confident that one day she will meet*
*One who will get her off her seat*

*No one less than her Mr. Darsy*
*Not specifically as fancy or classy*
*But most importantly being worthy*
*Respectfully treating her with mercy*

*Don't underestimate her dream*
*As fictional as it seems*
*She is simply a girl with standards*
*Incapable of healing heart cancers*

*He doesn't belong to an extinct specimen!*
*Just support her and say amen*
*When she prays to encounter him and then*
*Congratulate her over and over again.*

# Moribund

*Do you know who am I?*
*I am a cocoon with wings*
*No, I am not a butterfly*
*I am chained with golden wings*

*Yes, I don't fly*
*Though it seems I can*
*And I'll continue to deny*
*For, I have a short life span*

*Just a favor please!*
*That is all I ask*
*Untangle me with ease*
*That is not a difficult task*

*I'll die very soon*
*And I need to fly*
*Rest please, I am not heading to the moon*
*But towards a new place for my eye.*

# To My Haters

*To all the haters out there*
*Struggling to see my despair*
*Soon you'll be hearing my roar*
*You know I am made of titanium core*

*Is that what you really want to see?*
*A wrecked ship begging for mercy*
*Sorry, but mine is already sailing*
*And your conspiracies are fortunately failing*

*I am fortified against the treacherous wind*
*With compassion, love, and faith*
*So why don't you take a purity bath*
*And genuine values try to brace*

*Taylor has sung that haters are going to hate*
*But she forgot that they are sometimes your mates*
*Though it is never too late*
*To spit their poisonous bait.*

# A Tribute to a Friend

*You make the orders*
*And we are obliged to abide*
*No one has to cross your borders*
*Or he'll be set among those on the other side*
*A typical representation of contradiction*
*The reason why I am void of any familiar diction*
*To describe your sudden frustration*
*Or your overwhelming exhilaration*

*Don't get me wrong my dearest*
*I am aware my words sound as if you are the craziest*
*Well, you can be grouped among the weirdest*
*Possessing a heart tasting the sweetest*

*I was lonely eight years ago*
*But all of the sudden I found a new amigo*
*The first person to call me his best*
*And separated me from all of the rest*
*Making sorrow escapes out of my chest*

*You stood beside me through hardships*
*And backed me up overcoming obstacles*
*That was the secret ingredient of our friendship*
*One, strong enough to inspire an author while writing articles*

*And to many years to come*
*Don't let go of my band*
*I might seem content to some*
*Still, I need to visit your secret land.*

# Agony

*I reached rock bottom*
*That is what I figured out*
*When I started chasing your phantom*
*In the midst of a prolonged drought*

*You'll never be mine*
*But hopeful I'll remain*
*That at one time*
*I'll be able to break the chain*

*The one locking my heart*
*To be touched by another soul*
*It was yours from the start*
*It was yours as a whole*

*Now I am agonizing*
*For yours is with her*
*Her sight was mesmerizing*
*To your blind eyes for sure*

*But why was I ignored*
*By such a keen man*
*Wasn't my love something he can afford?*
*Or he thought I was just a fan?*

*No, he sensed my boiling blood*
*The blood burning his pride*
*But still I am waiting for a flood*
*To grow my soul into his mind.*

# Don't Settle for Less

*Don't settle for less*
*You're more than just an option*
*Erupt from your excess distress*
*And place your feelings out for auction*

*Wait for the highest bidder*
*Who's going to make you a trend on Twitter*
*Those who are ready to go over and beyond*
*And to your daily complaints, kindly respond*

*You're the first letter of the alphabet*
*The first number on the list*
*You're a French baguette and a vintage cassette*
*You're the most intricate narrative with a twist*

*Brace yourself in the meantime*
*And dig deeply into your soul mine*
*Unveil your hidden worth and talents*
*While residing in your favorite planets.*

# Lost Friendship

*That day I realized*
*That I no longer believe in love reciprocity*
*Obviously, all my feelings were fantasized*
*About your depth of love and its ferocity*

*You're neither my love, nor my brother*
*I thought you're my friend in need*
*Turned out you're my slow smother*
*And you fed your arrogance on my soul indeed*

*Your poker face says it all*
*Better though than your fake attention*
*Like you're wandering in a vast mall*
*While your credit card is on suspension*

*But I'll hold on to our friendship*
*Sailing in salty water as usual on our ship*
*Waiting eagerly to reach the safety of my land*
*Where pure water I am allowed to sip.*

# I No Longer Care

*I no longer care*
*For my feelings I'll start to share*

*I no longer care*
*For I am now willing to dare*

*I no longer care*
*For adversaries I am used to bear*

*I no longer care*
*For of my feelings you are unaware*

*I no longer care*
*Despite your ignorance of how I am rare*

*I no longer care*
*For I am invisible as breathed air*

*I no longer care*
*For I know 1 might spend my life solitaire*

*I no longer care*
*I no longer care.*

# A Daughter

*A beautiful lady she is*
*Shining all through the world*
*She keeps on blessing me with a kiss*
*But her words are fierce as a sword*

*A powerful character with a loud voice*
*Echoing all through the room*
*Though she is almost very close*
*To become a flower with a bloom*

*Her independence amazes my mind*
*But her temper has to be controlled*
*And a solution I am trying to find*
*So, a new technique got to be enrolled*

*I love her from all my heart*
*And wish her the best of everything*
*She is my precious piece of art*
*And to her I hope to be something*

*Or someone carved deep inside*
*For my tears will start dropping*
*If my love she'll set aside*
*And my name gets forgotten*

*Surely, she'll love my poem I assume*
*Because she is my beloved perfume.*

# Confusion

*And it is okay to be confused*
*When you have been living an illusion*
*For you will not be excused*
*To lead your soul into its execution*

*Like you can't decide what to wear*
*You are cold inside but the weather seems fair*
*You open the window for some fresh air*
*But the cold again wouldn't allow you to dare*

*Still you continue with your confusion*
*Wondering if it can be cured with some seclusion*
*And all you get is a conclusion*
*That your confusion is nothing but an illusion.*

# If Only

*If only rocks can speak*
*Truth will unravel*
*How most have reached the peak*
*Craving a new place to travel*

*If only eyes are read*
*Our world will be in silence*
*Our spirits will calmly be fed*
*With peace, love, and shyness*

*If only my words were not scarce*
*I would have expressed my feelings*
*I would have held onto a precious chance*
*For my wounds' aches I'll be healing*

*If only man can find a closure*
*To his unbearable vulnerabilities*
*So, his true color will find an exposure*
*Saying goodbye to complexities.*

# A Salad Dish

*A salad dish is my life*
*Cut piece by piece with a knife*

*Modeled by my fingers' blood*
*Fingers stained with some dark mud*

*An overwhelming mosaic sight*
*Which covers what the knife had to fight*

*Every day I taste something new*
*Sweet or sour I continue to chew*

*They say a salad is all what your body needs*
*I say a pinch of salt is important indeed*

*It might probably affect your blood pressure*
*But that's life, darling, it is not always fair weather!*

# Maturity

*You hit that age of change*
*Sprouting off your enclosed cage*
*You're nothing but a weed*
*Needless of a precious seed*

*You know you just cease to put up with shit*
*Your character, thoughts and dreams are just lit*
*That age of I am enough*
*Life couldn't be more rough*
*On the verge of why not! I will quit!*

*The age of chilling despair*
*Carelessness become an artistic fair*
*You're not supposed to click on share*
*You are certain no one would even care*

*Instead you click on the cleansing button*
*You group your acquaintances by the dozen*
*When they choose to disappear all of a sudden*
*That age where all of their memories are forgotten*
*You're left with just a few to keep loving.*

# Lebanon

*My people's life has been paused*
*While their demands are being mocked*
*A national chaos has been caused*
*A dead end awaits us, don't be shocked!*

*Their billions have been already transferred*
*So, others' economies are now pampered*
*Their riches are now obviously laundered*
*Their rule won't soon change, it's standard*

*The revolution's motto is absolutely surreal*
*Try to listen to reason, just once, for real*
*We're upon a huge disaster, don't try to conceal*
*The conspiracies nest in every corner, listen dear*

*We have despised their rotten policies for years*
*You people spent ages governed by your fears*
*Cheering here and there about our country's souvenirs*
*So, in this occasion lend me your ears.*

*You allowed these funguses to absorb your wealth*
*And enclose you in a lengthy labyrinth*
*Attached to their thrones as Macbeth*
*Offering nothing but an ugly death*

*No harm in a human rights fight*
*Blocking the roads though isn't quite right*
*Think of a way to remove them out of your sight*
*So a new dawn might appear after a long night.*

# Growing Up

*Watching people here and there*
*Bitching about how life is unfair*

*I know one who is out there*
*Trying to collect somethings to share*

*He found nothing in the process*
*Claiming nothing was available to access*

*He lost connection through his journey*
*His purpose has no longer a definite scenery*

*He reconnected though with his long-time friend*
*Their relation wasn't meant yet to reach an end*

*Oh desperation let me try to amend*
*Your story traveled from land to land*

*My apologies your secret wasn't safe with me*
*I was weak in front of wicked trickery*

*Your memory they tried to overshadow*
*By opening the brightest luminous window*

*But your image remained always reflected*
*Which made sure I wasn't going to be affected*

*With your companionship I'll remain sane*
*We will have a long, long reign.*

# Stopped

*She can't find a solution*
*For her so long misery*
*Her plan was about to come to fruition*
*And it was stopped by his chivalry*

*She is not the villain in the story*
*Nor is he*
*His loyalty was the ultimate jury*
*And no witness had a clue*

*That she waited for years*
*With no substantial fears*
*She believed she was apt*
*To take advantage of the fact*
*That the other was no longer here*
*And his heart shall adapt*
*So, her heartbeat he'll start to hear*

*Disappointment is what she received*
*His loyalty was his master chief*
*The other one's heart was eventually retrieved*
*Making her nothing but a thief*

*She didn't believe in fairytales*
*But their story was one*
*The prince got united with the princess*
*Next to a lake full of swans*
*Ushering the time for her ship to sail*
*Loaded with indescribable distress*

*Forgive her when she turns her sight*
*Foe she is on her healing journey*
*Where her desires she ought to fight*
*Treating them mercilessly*
*Although her eyes are forbidden from his sight*
*He'll always have a special residence in her heart.*

# Chill

*Emotions are meant to be expressed*
*However, some are better being suppressed*
*Your overreaction renders everyone upset*
*Darling we're altogether already overstressed*

*Your Su casa isn't my Mi casa*
*Give us a break and cut off the drama*
*It is not like you're residing in Gaza*
*Control yourself until you're with your momma*

*You look fake when you start to shake*
*Go and try a piece of chocolate cake*
*Or clean your shit with mamma's long rake*
*I beg you... for our sake.*

# Lost Humanity

*Hello my fellow human brother*
*I've got no intention to really brother*
*I've just arrived here to question*
*Your sustainable racism session*

*Now, my first would be the simplest*
*Are you authorized to run a lecture?*
*Guess not, been told you're among the dumbest*
*Whose brains unsupported knowledge pressure*

*And my second is not of much difference*
*Yet, it delivers a valuable inference*
*Are you his neighbor and friend in labor?*
*Ahhh, wait, wait I will ask the mayor*

*Indeed, he replied in the same language*
*But asked me to help you carry the luggage*
*Of a likewise DNA holders*
*And drive them straight through the borders*
*Knowing you share common ancestors*

*Blindfolded with hatred and weakness*
*Lost contact with your inner human feelings*
*Restore your good ethics and kindness*
*Hold my words like permanent earrings.*

# 2020

*Always grateful for God's blessings*
*The world is a mess, very upsetting*
*Everyone is reacting by just guessing*
*What went wrong! Utterly depressing*

*God is watching our despicable deeds*
*Wars are all around us while we're scrolling over our*
*Facebook feeds*
*Our problems are becoming sarcastic memes*
*No one gives a shit about others, it seems*

*We're spiritually corrupted: me, myself and I*
*I want to help others, what a big lie!!!*
*Repent and help yourself first*
*Confess that you're in your sins, immersed*

*Whether a fire, a war, or a virus*
*Pick up what you're mostly afraid of, plus or minus*
*Always remember God is the most merciful*
*Start with yourself, undoubtedly, it's fruitful*
*Don't forget to always be thankful*
*Alhamdulillah, by God's will, will make you successful.*

# Game of Thrones

*The greatest show ever made*
*Has recently received a lot of shade*
*It turned into a precious goods to trade*
*And its glamour started slowly to fade*

*An honest message to all the loyal fans*
*You don't get to choreograph the show's dance*
*Your esteemed writer didn't grab the chance*
*To finish the books and the plot enhance*

*Watching GOT has sabotaged your mind*
*Academic scholars you are! One of a kind*
*Your criticism has become a source to cite*
*Relax Mr. and Mrs., right!!!*

*I enjoyed every bit of the season*
*D&D's writing is the main reason*
*What they did isn't at all a high treason*
*Without them there wouldn't be a throne*
*They literally have made be overblown!*

# Sister

*My one and only sister*
*My confident and wise minister*
*The embodiment of depression*
*And inner feelings' suppression*

*I am writing to ask you a favor*
*Stop being your soul slaver*
*We know you're an undiscovered gem*
*Embrace your dazzling colors and don't care about them*

*Those who undermine your worth*
*Love yourself and keep going forth*
*You're not chained as you believe*
*Lots of work ahead of you! So, roll up your sleeve*

*I can't share some of your agony, yet I understand*
*You feel you're being built and destroyed like a snowman*
*So vulnerable and fragile*
*Residing alone in a cold and harsh exile*

*Winter doesn't last forever though*
*Your morale wouldn't remain always low*

*The sun will shine and your flowers will grow*
*The crop of your parenting you will gladly sow*

*A gorgeous mother you are*
*Stop pouring alcohol onto your scare!*
*Take care of your grounded fruitful tree*
*Rest assured you're always going to have a friend in me.*

# Nephew

*You wrote me two days ago*
*And I cheered when I sighted your hello*
*I love you tremendously, you know!*
*And I seek your reciprocal also*

*I am aware you're not a big fan of my attitude*
*You think I am sometimes rude*
*Or an aunt with swings in her mood*
*But your opinion of me has to be reviewed*

*To my first nephew I say*
*We were exhilarated on your birthday*
*Even if we might yell when you overplay*
*And ask you to stop straightaway*

*But I want you to be the best in the world*
*A clever man you are! Still unexplored*
*I am certain you are on your pathway towards*
*Being a famous champion holding many awards.*

*I am not a control freak as you think*
*I am overprotective, just an instinct*
*It isn't refreshing though, just like mint*
*But my love is hard just like zinc.*

# Leave Me

*Leave me be, I'll be okay*
*I am absolutely positive, not a cliché*
*I got the results of my in-depth survey*
*Whatever you say, is all the shades of grey*

*Leave me be, and get lost!*
*Your presence has an expensive cost*
*Drinking your toxic venom, gradually, in shots*
*You take me for granted, by default*
*A lesson was taught, though it's my fault*

*Leave me be, I'll definitely be well*
*I'm out of my comfort zone, have broken the shell Imprisoned*
*in your zone, obscure as hell*
*"Never mind, I'll find someone like you," as chanted by Adel*
*In a more liberating dwelling, where I'll flaunt as a gazelle.*

*Leave me be, I wish to own back my peace*
*And collect the shreds of my feelings, piece by piece.*

# Battle

*Everyone is fighting his own battle*
*While trying to set himself on his saddle*

*You can judge a book by its cover*
*But never a man undercover*
*As a happy fellow full of joy*
*Altered to a senseless plastic toy*

*You think you carry the heaviest burden*
*And your ship is the only one already sunken*
*Your inner core is totally molten*
*My dear, your prejudice is completely rotten*

*Because everyone is fighting his own battle*
*You know our battles might be different*
*You might be in desperation, fluent*
*Whilst my life is enormously ruined*
*Tackling my problems by being silent.*

*Because everyone is fighting his own battle*
*Your war is not the most unprecedented matter*
*It's all about life choices*
*Shall we keep it to ourselves or sing it in a chorus?*

# Thoughts

*Thought I've grown*
*Read too much about self-love*
*About peace of mind, about gratitude*
*All incorporated into my core*
*Wasn't reflected though in much fortitude*

*Thought I've grown*
*Embedding self-care on a daily basis*
*Dealing with circumstances without much analysis*
*Flying carelessly as light as foam*

*Thought I've grown*
*Still I need your validation*
*I need your approval and encouragement*
*I can't run without your admiration*
*Or else, I all agonize from abandonment*
*I might not deserve all of this attention*
*Sadly, I still need it for my contention.*

# Heavy Heart

*I am sick with a heavy heart*
*Waiting for something presumably chosen to depart*

*Searching for an antidote*
*An immunity vaccine to decipher the ache's code*
*To lubricate this motionless machine*

*Can't bear the constant pain*
*Words are no longer soothing the strain*
*Not asking for anyone's aid*
*I'll be heading soon on a crusade*
*I'll claim my potion, I'll eradicate the pain*
*Wish me a successful campaign*
*To exterminate this toxic corrosion.*

# Misunderstood

*I amok with being misunderstood*
*It's okay if I don't belong to your hood*
*Too many hardships I've withstood*
*I don't need you, I buy my own food*

*I'll overlook your hypersensitivity*
*I now seek constant tranquility*
*Your emotions are no longer my priority*
*I can peacefully live with our incompatibility*

*No extra effort will be granted*
*Nor your empathy is demanded*
*Trust me, I can't thrive by being stranded*
*I'll move on until my rhymes are chanted.*

# Attitude

*Your social behavior is interchangeable*
*Introverted, extroverted, they're all labels*
*Let your attitude become debatable*
*When they judge you, just turn the tables*

*Tell them it's all a reflection of their actions*
*Their nature, efforts and practices*
*Don't you dare entice me to mention*
*Your neglect, discouragement, and core damages*

*No place for you in my narrow circle*
*Our correspondence would be restricted on being verbal.*

*Go ahead and question our relation*
*I perceive it as a complicated obligation*

*Where my true feelings can't genuinely be articulated Though*
*your fake energy will most likely be simulated.*

# Patience

Good driving is never enough
To reach your destination
Way too many other stuff
Along a trip to the gas station

It isn't as thrilling as Cruise's missions
Though definitely worth the effort
May require a faithful escort
To ensure some noticeable progression

What is missing though
Is self-approval
Which in my case is very low

Prejudices are holding me hanging
And opportunities are passing me by, waving
So, it is about time to use my car's breaks
For I am excellent at driving
I got all what it really takes.

# Tough

*Some people are just tough*
*Whatever you do, their treatment remains rough*

*A discussion with them causes a concussion*
*Whatever you utter has an awful repercussion*

*See, I am not a low or flat microwave muffin*
*I rise, and I'll start dealing with you as a Russian*

*I don't care who you are!*
*Stop acting like a radar*
*It's not appealing to be that bizarre*
*You're far away from being a rock star*

*You're a strong headed know-it-all!*
*Lower down your gaze, you might hit a wall*
*Or may tumble down with your evil eyeball*
*No one would help you, above all*
*They despise your attitude all in all…*

# Healing Journey

*Since when I lost my attachment*
*To your approval, my pathetic refuel*
*Since I detached from your enchantment*
*Which was futile and utterly cruel*

*Since when I hated you so fiercely*
*Hated your words, lies, and excuses*
*They seemed to be impeccably princely*
*Well chosen and articulated, yet deemed abuses*

*Since when I vibe solo*
*I enjoy my own company!*
*Since I realized I must not be treated so low*
*By someone worth not more than a penny*

*Now I feel much better*
*For I have been, for so long, bitter*
*I learned a valuable lesson however*
*You sucked life out of me, it was a huge error*
*I'll mend my soul, I'll be fond of life's pleasures!*

# The Sun will Rise

*The sun will keep on rising the next day*
*Even if you blew things up being a prey*
*Of your overthinking and anxiety*
*And all the triviality of our corrupted society*

*The sun will keep on rising the next day*
*Even if they judged you while being away*
*Taking care and loving yourself*
*And to life's atrocities, playing deaf*

*The sun will keep on rising the next day*
*When things don't necessarily run your way*
*You can stop playing by the rules*
*Leads to nothing but a change in moods!*

*The sun will keep on rising the next day*
*After your heartbreak, and it's okay*
*Remove assumptions and expectations*
*Alter them to realistic aspirations*

*The sun will keep on rising the next day*
*Sway darling, even if the skies are gray*

*A high chance you'll receive some of its rays*
*Just hold on and appreciate any delays.*

# Vibing Solo

*I am in a current state of loneliness*
*Surrounded by many, yet I feel homeless*
*Do excuse me if I seemed a bit hopeless*
*Think I have hit a new level of lowness*

*I am in no need of your company*
*You're just not enough for me honey*
*You're no one but a 'somebody'*
*I spend time with, reluctantly*

*For I really have no one special*
*I try to conceal it, but it's detrimental*
*I believe it is no longer confidential*
*I miss the part where I was sentimental*

*Where everything was significant*
*And I was to your feelings, considerate*
*But now I am blank, literally illiterate*
*So I'll retreat, I won't be a participant.*

# Accusations

*When they accuse you of being cold hearted*
*Tell them your boundaries are now undistorted*
*You have just become more mature*
*You don't dress mediocrely, you aim for couture*

*Traveling abroad is not the reason*
*It's not a matter of a region or a season*
*It is mainly the way you now use to reason*
*Manifesting the exorcism of your own demon*

*You are now more established*
*Your life long worries are almost banished*
*You only strive for peace and balance*
*You truly are your desired gallant*

*Let their accusations hunt them*
*You are out of their league, so let them condemn*
*You are now living in a different realm*
*Surrounding yourself with genuine gems.*